In *Manhattan Moments*, Rosalie Calabrese sings it as she sees it. An unstoppable observer and channeler of urban inner life (the Big Apple variety), she puts words together like frames of a film — a cinematographer with a pencil — taking us with her as she sneaks into the nooks and crannies that lead to a life's rich store of feelings. She is a single woman but not a solo act. She's married to Manhattan.

— BRUCE FAGIN, VICE PRESIDENT,
THE GOOD DOG FOUNDATION

Rosalie Calabrese's deliciously insightful new poetry collection, *Manhattan Moments*, juxtaposes opposites, confounding assumptions about the city you think you know. Her first poem, "A Page from My Diary," describes a sidewalk meet-up and then drops you off at a very unexpected destination (under a smoky haloed moon). "Eavesdropping," set in a sandwich shop, is a humorous gem of aperçu, while "City Poet," a stylistic wonder, shows nature up against asphalt. Perhaps my favorite, both amusing and captivating in its upbeat melancholy, "On the 72nd Street Crosstown" makes you feel without yanking your heartstrings.

— CAROLINE THOMAS, FOUNDER & DIRECTOR,
TOTAL THEATRE LAB

Manhattan Moments

Also by Rosalie Calabrese

Remembering Chris
Hoboken, NJ: Poets Wear Prada, 2015

Zine workers
with Mark Sonnenfeld
East Windsor, NJ: Marymark Press, 2010

A Few Poems for Hard Times
New York, NY: Katydid Press, 2009

Growing Up Jewish
New York, NY: Katydid Press, 2005

In Print
New York, NY: Katydid Press, 2002

Writer's Choice
New York, NY: Katydid Press, 2000

Manhattan Moments

poems by

Rosalie Calabrese

POETS WEAR PRADA • Hoboken, New Jersey

Manhattan Moments

Poets Wear Prada
533 Bloomfield Street, Second Floor
Hoboken, New Jersey 07030
http://pwpbooks.blogspot.com

First North American Publication 2020
First Mass Market Paperback Edition 2020

Grateful acknowledgment is made to the following publications where some of these poems have previously appeared:

And Then, *Big City Lit*, *Brownstone Poets Anthology*, *The Dramatists Guild Quarterly*, *Emerson of Harvard* (Quill Books), *First Literary East*, *Muses Run on the Subway Tracks* (Jaroslav E. Sykora), *Nebu*, *The New York Times*, *Poetry in Performance*, and *Thirteen Poetry Magazine*.

ISBN-13: 978-0-9979811-4-8
ISBN-10: 0-9979811-4-8

Library of Congress Control Number: 2018944455

Printed in the U.S.A.

Front Cover & Title Pages: James Morgan
Author Photo: Renee Conly

To the city of my dreams

We'll have Manhattan.

— RODGERS & HART, 1925

Table of Contents

Manhattan Moments

A PAGE FROM MY DIARY
GOING HOME: NEW YORK CITY, 1989

One block from home, that last mile
of a midsummer night's reality,
twisted shadows dance
to the beat of my thumping heart.

I brandish a lighted cigarette,
attack the pavement
in the tempo
set by a woman up ahead.

Our footsteps echo
in friendly synchrony
until she turns
to enter a building.

Deserter!

But it's okay;
here comes a patrol car.
I hum "Here Comes the Sun"
and quicken my pace.

At the intersection of WALK & DON'T WALK,
I defy traffic
to reach the safety of my own turf.
I take a slow drag
on the half-smoked cigarette
and smile at an oncoming stranger.

"Got another one?" he asks.
I damn the price of them,

search a dimly lit face
for signs of danger.

"Don't be afraid," he says.
"I won't do you any harm.
One cigarette's all I want,
and then I'm gone."

"Hey," I respond boldly,
"I stopped for you, didn't I?"

Handing him the pack,
I dig inside my bag
to find a match,
but he's impatient.

"I'll take it off of yours,"
he says, his hand on mine.
My smoldering ember
starts his fire. A smoky halo
encircles the moon.

2 A.M.

Take a cab, my friends urged.
Nah, I'll be home in no time, I said,
grinning as the uptown bus came into view.
Taking a window seat, I pulled out some scribbles
and reconsidered where I wanted them to go.

34th Street. I crossed out the first two lines . . .
59th. The words were looking fuzzy . . .
Okay, 72nd. Just a few stops more . . .
I opened one eye and squinted at the sign outside.
125th. A HUNDRED AND TWENTY-FIFTH!

Standing in the street, trying not to panic —
no people, no cars,
no subway nearby —
do I dare walk the thirty blocks I missed?
But whoa — a taxi cab!

Forcing myself to stay awake,
I watch the numbers on the meter jump:
$5, 7.50, 9. *Far corner, right side*,
thinking how pleased my friends would be
to know I took a cab.

AT THE RUSH HOUR

Pursued by Murphy's Law, running late
for an appointment I should have canceled,
I miss the express and curse the minutes . . .
while the local crawls . . . towards 42nd Street.

There, a teenager — faded jeans, sneakers,
hair pulled into a ponytail;
her eyes closed as in a classic statue —
navigates the crowd, led by a service dog.

On the stairs, stumbling in my rush, I see
the girl and her guide — calm, sure-footed —
move ahead into the waning light outside,
lifting the bleakness of my day as they go.

IS THIS A JOKE?

Is this a joke, or what?

I'm standing on the subway —
Fifty-some years old
With dried-up ovaries
And a batch of false teeth —
Trying to focus on the book
In your hand — Pynchon, no less —
While my trifocals magnify
The bulge in your pants.

As the train lurches forward,
My juices reawaken with a start.

If you could read my thoughts,
Would you laugh?

OF TWO MINDS
A[nother] Subway Story

". . . dumped out of my apartment,"
she tells the guy she enters with,
her back against the closing doors.
"How awful," he says, shifting his weight.
"Whatever —" she shrugs as the train
begins to move and drowns her out.

I dare not ask if no place to sleep
is just a petty annoyance,
like missing the train
or the spiel of a person
who begs for money
you know will go for booze.

Of two minds, the sweet me
and the soured one, I make a bet
on whether he'll take her in
or, smelling a ploy,
say goodbye at the next station.
I get off; he doesn't.

Lacking a coin to flip,
in need of an ending,
I turn to my book
and read the last page:
They move in together.
But I think it's a big mistake.

EAVESDROPPING

"Counting everything,"
the guy at a nearby table tells his friend,
"trip only cost me a thou. . . .

. . . lay of the land . . .
volleyball . . . aerobics . . .
new friend . . .
wired Mom for money . . .
bailed out . . . "

Vacation, I think.
"Jail," I hear him say.

I bite into my sandwich, wonder
if next time he'll get such a good deal.

THE SECOND SHOW

Outside the theater just before eight.
Old ladies wearing Reeboks
Jostle past the last-minute smokers
As if they see an empty seat on the subway
While ad agency types in suits & ties
Hair slicked back in '50s fashion
Carry on a sophisticated patter
Loud enough to be overheard
By the stonewashed Levi's crowd
That huddles near the pudgy men
Sporting houndstooth jackets and flannel slacks
Who have helped spangled, beaded princesses
Out of rented limousines.
As we surge through the doors
In response to a warning
That the curtain is going up,
I become aware of a conversation nearby:
"My mother says we have to see *Falsettos*."
"She really liked it, huh?"
"Oh, yeah, she's a sucker for bar mitzvahs."
We find our seats, the lights dim
And the second show begins.

FOOD FOR THOUGHT

Crossing 14th Street at Second Avenue,
my friend John and I spot a Nathan's,
famous for its Coney Island hot dogs,
with a sign above the door — 2 FOR $2.
We go in and order the bargain meal,
mustard & sauerkraut no extra charge.

On our way out
I hear a teenager say to his date:
"You don't want to know
how sausage is made;
it's really disgusting."

The taste of hot dog still in my mouth,
I remember a film
from high school biology
about Pepsi Cola rotting your stomach,
which — even after fifty years —
has kept me from having a soda.

COMPARATIVE RELIGION

Stuck in the tunnel between 34th and 42nd,
I suddenly find myself alone on the subway.

No metaphysical revelation,
this reality grinds in my gut
like the gears of the immobilized train.

The adjacent cars offer safety in numbers,
but gripped by indecision, rooted to the spot,

I sway left to right as if in a Talmudic trance
and pray that a crazed panhandler
doesn't barge in to prove my descent from Job.

Sorry for the inconvenience. . . .
God's message over the loudspeaker
signals absolution, kick-starts the motor.

Not given to genuflection,
I take a deep breath and count my blessings.

SUBWAY ANGEL

Amplified guitar instead of wings,
Her voice mellow as earth after rain,
She wails "Stand by Me"
With a pure country twang.

I look up from my book to see
People dancing on the platform!
First one couple, then another,
Then we're all moving to the beat.

The train shimmies into the station
And grinds to a stop; so do we.
No time to leave a tip, still
She blesses me with a smile.

ON THE LOWER EAST SIDE

Native New Yorkers
by way of Queens and Brooklyn,
my love and I found our dream apartment —
well, affordable — on E. 10th & Second.
Finding a working phone booth
in front of the Second Avenue Deli,
I called my parents with the good news.
"OH, NO," Daddy cried. "That's where
I lived right off the boat!
If you move there, I won't visit."
He said no more . . .
Now I ride the subway
to the vintage boutique on E. 12th
and imagine memories he never shared.

INVITATION

I was in the shower —
Water a perfect temperature, hair full of suds —
Naturally, the phone rang.
Let it go, I told myself,
That's why God made answering machines.

Still — dripping with more than curiosity —
I ran to retrieve the message.

"Hi," said an unfamiliar voice,
"This is Monica, 212-blah-blah-blah.
I guess your father didn't tell you
I'm getting married on Friday.
We're having a dinner
At the Kosher Chinese restaurant
Next to the Telephone Bar in the East Village.

"Please call me . . . I'm really happy . . .
And no, I'm not pregnant."

Delighted, I dialed the number and got her machine.
"Hello," I said. "You don't know me
So I don't think I should come to your wedding,
But thanks for the invitation . . . and
Congratulations!"

ROACHES

I used to smoke them but quit
after a bad batch of hash
made me think I was dying.

I used to kill them — dozens —
the kind that came down in droves
from the slob who lived upstairs.

Now, as I look back,
I see how much in life
takes on more than one meaning.

CITY POET

Knowing full well that nature
Is the seed of many a great poem,
I still search the streets to pick ideas
I hope will blossom into golden phrases.

In a local store I pluck a set of dishes,
Each cup and plate
Patterned with a delicate flower —
Decals pasted on to look like the real thing.

Back outside, I contemplate weeds
Growing through cracks in the concrete.

CENTRAL PARK AFTER A SNOWSTORM

Ballerinas in white, the trees
bend their snow-clad limbs
to take a bow

in this moment of ecstatic silence

before the chorus of traffic horns
returns to honk its applause.

FIRE

2 a.m. Sirens and alarms.
A stench like burnt feathers
at the chicken flicker's
when I was a kid.

Whorls of gray smoke in the hallway.
Grab the mink, warm slippers,
cigarettes, eyeglasses.
Leave the purse. To hell with it.

Out on the terrace, all's quiet
except for the parade of fire engines
sixteen floors below. Even with a net,
would I have the guts to jump?

"Fire, fire," I yell into the dark.
"Isn't anybody home?"
The cigarette I light is dizzying
like the first puff after surgery.

Finally, another glow:
my neighbor on fifteen
whose daughter won't let her
smoke in the house.

"It's the compactor room," she calls to me.
"Don't open your front door;
put a towel down
to keep the smoke out."

Exhausted as I am,
I follow her orders
and hear the firemen

on walkie-talkies.

Bypassing the Bailey's
saved for a special occasion,
taking seltzer instead,
I raise my glass to the brave men in the hall.

Later I dream that my child —
a hermaphrodite named Queenie
with ice cream hair,
chocolate-dipped braids

tucked into a soldier's cap —
has returned from war.
My arms thrown around it,
the apparition melts away.

Morning. The hallway's clear.
I pick up my newspaper as usual,
only a faint odor to remind me
there are things I can never imagine.

AFTER A MONTH
OCTOBER 2001

From behind my bedroom window,
I watched a fire down the street last night.
Like 9/11, on TV, it drew me in.
Even so, I saw the irony:
9/11 without its slash is 911.
Now I hear there's anthrax in the mail —
fear out of 911's control.
No longer feeling safe at home,
far from dangers *over there*,
I look for humor in despair.

MID-JULY AFTER DARK

Out on the terrace —
my glasses left inside,
astigmatism turns
streetlights to sparklers;

air conditioners,
in a thousand windows,
thrum backup for the
pulse of Manhattan;

a phantom breeze delivers
an old lover's kiss,
overdue but still welcome;
no fire engines, no ambulances,

no revving motorcycles,
not even one angry car alarm
or low-flying plane
to break the mood.

My windows are open;
I'll sleep well tonight.

PHANTOM TRAIN

Southbound, its final stop unmarked,
the train that ran beside us
suddenly is gone.

It can't be the one over there,
moving back on the Manhattan-bound track
while we're stopped, here, at Metrotech.

I saw that train, I swear!
It must be somewhere — on Earth
. . . or elsewhere

TENTH AVENUE

Leaving the relative safety of an M11 bus,
I enter unfamiliar territory
where my senses are accosted by music
blaring from a TV repair shop,
and a bleached-blond transvestite
grabs a black Latino of indeterminate sex
to salsa-fy her bump-and-grind swivel.
I think I should cross the street
but, pulled by the magnetic pulse,
I join in their dance
without concern for the look of things.

ON THE 72ND STREET
   CROSSTOWN

Watching an elderly man and woman
dressed alike in black & white,
heads nodding, simultaneously,
in commuter half-sleep,
I thought how lovely it must be
to grow old together.

At Madison Avenue, as she got off
and he stayed on without goodbyes,
I thought of my parents
not speaking to each other
for their last ten years . . .

and why I still spoke to my ex
after he left without a goodbye.

AUTUMN SOLSTICE

We've lit the candles; said the kaddish,
"Yisgadal v'yiskadash . . .";
shed the tears; then broken the fast.
With my head still full of prayers,
I walk to Supercuts, along a street
where the trees have not yet shed their leaves.

The woman who cuts my hair
asks me what I want
but doesn't follow my instructions.
At the house, dinner is late.
I wait an hour for the next bus
back to New York.

On the C train headed uptown,
a young man kneels before the signboard,
spinning and spinning the panels
that show the final destination.
He stops at P.
I wonder if he knows where he's going.

I wonder if P
is a better place than home.

THE WAKE-UP CALL

Good morning, ladies and gentlemen,
my name is Mary / John / Alice . . .
oh, never mind . . .
I'm homeless / battered / blind / lame /
hungry / cold / tired; victim of
AIDS / poverty / discrimination . . .
take your pick.
Good morning, you subway slouchers
tuning out the noise, the dirt,
the crowd, and the likes of me.
I don't ask for food or money,
haven't got a thing to sell.
But damn it, look me in the eye
while you're sitting on my bed!

CUT FLOWER

Last night I replaced the dried-out roses
on my dining table, by the window,
with a fresh tulip, brought home
from a friend's birthday party,
and set the bud's pink head
to face my chair.

This morning the Brooklyn baby
plucked from his dead mother,
in yesterday's front-page hit-and-run,
is reported also dead; the flower,
newly opened, has turned
to face the sky.

AFTER THE STORM

We all admit to feeling guilty, those of us
filling the streets this Halloween night,
which feels more ghostly for the lack of costumes
or kids out in packs trick-or-treating,
here on the Upper West Side, where Sandy,
the mega storm that took down half the city
and surrounding areas, left us pretty much intact.

Coming from a restaurant
that's almost out of everything on the menu,
squished together on a bus
that can only take on as many people as get off,
we talk to strangers
about luck and prospects for our future,
as if there were anything we could do
about any of it.

HOMETOWN HAIKU

A homeless woman
sleeping where the flowers bloom
behind a wire fence

❀

The LIRR
A Friday night in summer
Standing room only

❀

New Year's revelers
fill Times Square on my TV
I change the channel

❀

Walking the High Line
6 a.m. Sunday morning
Not even church bells

❀

Off to Mexico
Flying out of JFK
Hasta la vista.

❀

WALKING DOWN BROADWAY

Just before sundown
on the fifth day of a heat wave,
I slog past a loose-limbed senior
singing into his cellphone
"I Just Called to Say I love You."
Presuming there's a woman on the other end,
I wonder if she's laughing or just
soaking up love like a warm bath.
A few blocks later, at Sabon,
I take a fleeting glance
through the plate glass window.
There, among the soaps and body butter,
two young women are dancing, each one
slathered in her own frenetic motions.
My reactions gel and joy bubbles up
as I bop on down the street.

YELLOW CABS

Like glowing neon whales,
Schools of yellow cabs
With dark cushiony bellies
Bearing dreams of warm caresses
Swim along the rainswept street
While I stand stranded beneath
A leaky hotel awning,
Watching an off-duty driver
Stop for someone else.
Madly waving a soggy *Playbill*,
As my prayers and curses intermingle,
I slosh through sooty puddles
And sound the urban war cry:
TAXI!

STILL AN ADVENTURE

When I was twelve,
taking the Jamaica Avenue El
an hour away from Queens
to Manhattan was like going
to my own adventure park,
even before such things existed.

As I walk today to the Cooper Hewitt
at 91st & Fifth — Central Park across
the way, staidly green above
its wall of rough-hewn stone —
a sudden gust of wind makes
confetti of the pansies and wildflowers
hung in planters on the buildings to my left.

After the conference on Art & Computers
that brought me to Andrew Carnegie's house,
I follow a docent up the elegant marble stairs,
perfectly preserved amid the carved oak walls —
yet another surprise in the city of
a twelve-year-old's dreams.

❋

Acknowledgments

The author extends her thanks to the following publications where some of these poems first appeared, sometimes under a different title or in a slightly different format:

Big City Lit	"ROACHES"
Brownstone Poets Anthology	"WALKING DOWN BROADWAY"
The Dramatists Guild Quarterly	"THE SECOND SHOW," "YELLOW CABS"
Emerson of Harvard: a Celebrative Bicentennial Anthology to Ralph Waldo Emerson (1803–1882), Quill Books, 2003	"SUBWAY ANGEL"
First Literary Review	"EAVESDROPPING"
Muses Run on the Subway Tracks, Jaroslav E. Sykora, 2018	"OF TWO MINDS"
Nebo: A Literary Journal	"FOOD FOR THOUGHT"
The New York Times (Metropolitan Diary, City Room)	"2 A.M.," "CENTRAL PARK AFTER A SNOWSTORM," "HOMETOWN HAIKU"
Poetry in Performance	"AT THE RUSH HOUR," "CITY POET," "TENTH AVENUE," "ON THE 72ND STREET CROSSTOWN"
Thema	"A PAGE FROM MY DIARY"
Thirteen Poetry Magazine	"IS THIS A JOKE?"

"COMPARATIVE RELIGION" first appeared in the author's book *Growing Up Jewish*. "IS THIS A JOKE" was previously reprinted in *And Then* magazine.

About the Author

Rosalie Calabrese is the author of *Remembering Chris* (Poets Wear Prada, 2015) as well as five other books of poetry. Among her nearly one hundred publication credits are *Cosmopolitan*, *The New York Times*, *Jewish Currents*, and *Mom Egg Review*. Frequently anthologized, her work has appeared in several bestselling collections edited by June Cotner, some published by Center Street (an imprint of Hachette), others by Broadway Books and Harmony Books (imprints of the Crown Publishing Group owned by Penguin Random House). Rosalie's poems have been set to music as art songs by Eugene McBride, Francis Thorne, Leonard Lehrman, Joel Suben, and others. She has collaborated on musicals, writing librettos, with Anthony Calabrese, Francis James Brown, and Blair Weille.

A native New Yorker who works as a management consultant for the arts, she previously held the position of Executive Director of American Composers Alliance. In that capacity, she helped to establish the highly esteemed American Composers Orchestra and served on its original board of directors. Her current clients include pianists Margaret Mills and Patricia Garcia-Torres, composer and poet Mira Spektor, composer/poet/performance artist Marni Rice, and conductor Roit Feldenkreis.

Rosalie's professional affiliations include BMI (Broadcast Music, Inc.), PEN America, and The Dramatists Guild.

About the Artist

James Morgan has been associated with The York Theatre Company for 44 years, the last 21 as Producing Artistic Director. He has designed scenery for over 300 productions in theaters around the country. Recently: *Cagney* (York, Westside Theatre, El Portal); *Finian's Rainbow* (Irish Rep); *Born Yesterday* (St. Louis Rep); *Vanya and Sonia and Masha and Spike* (Peterborough; NH Theatre Award); *Unexpected Joy*, *Desperate Measures*, *Marry Harry* (Henry Hughes nomination). Currently: *On A Clear Day* (Irish Rep); *Lonesome Blues* (York). His graphic designs grace posters and CDs and the new scores and vocal selections of *Closer Than Ever* and *Merrily We Roll Along*, among others.

ABOUT THE TYPE

From the city that never sleeps, love calls. The Statue of Liberty beckons; 8.6 million (and growing) hearts welcome. Long Island, Hudson County, and Upstate New York join in to chant the mantra; new arrivals respond in kind.

When the New York State Department of Economic Development sought slogan, jingle, and logo to capture the essence, evoke appropriate appreciation, and help metamorphose the moribund metropolis of the nineteen seventies to erstwhile preeminence as the Big Apple, ♣, ♦, and ♠ folded, trumped in high-stakes play for the city's maiden hand. In the back of a yellow cab, Milton Glaser had scribbled — in red crayon on white envelope — three letters and the outline of a heart. His feel-good doodle became official logo then viral meme:

I ♥
N Y

And just in time. It was 1977, and help was desperately needed to resuscitate an abandoned, shuttered city and its seven million (and shrinking) broken hearts. (A million had already fled, some driven to escape by escalating crime rate and racial tension, others simply pushed out by unprecedented economic downturn.)

Helvetica (the impossibly tidy typeface ubiquitous at the time), Caslon (the epitome of belletristic sophistication), Times New Roman (collared and tied) quietly withdrew from competition, ensconced in separate limousines.

Glaser's choice of typeface (and ours), American Typewriter, rose to the occasion, ascending *New York* magazine co-founder's now internationally famous logo. Allusively stacked typography, perched emoticon radiant beside the I's city spire rising above the borough / city / state monogram, presaged scaffolding to come and crested common cabs coursing through the increased traffic like the coiffures of Broadway stars emerging from stage doors into the gathered crowds. Visible, too, if more humbly, on the subway, it proclaimed love underground for the revitalized city and its inhabitants.

Homage to the machine that, until just recently, had served to implement Gotham's carbon imprint and reputation as a place for writers — Damon Runyon, Dorothy Parker, Joe Mitchell, and Fred (the hero-narrator of *Breakfast at Tiffany's*) among the many — American Typewriter adapted the distinctive serif typographers indecorously call "slab" (like those obituaries prepared for the still alive), long favored for display and increased legibility at diminished point size in advertising and journalism, a shape that nicely relates to the residual architecture of a bygone Manhattan: the sills and lintels of its great hotels, prewar apartments, private clubs, and public buildings.

Joel Kadan's and Tony Stan's 1974 design, published by Linotype, owned by International Typeface Corporation, abandoned the more common uniform spacing of the mechanical classic to embrace the proportional spacing enabled by the IBM Model B Executive Electric Typewriter. Kadan designed the light and medium styles of American Typewriter; Stan designed the bold. Maintaining diachronic pace with the digital age, Ed Bengulat added his italic version in 1979.

* * *

The cursive swirls of Shelly Allegro, similar to those employed by both New York baseball teams — the Yankees and the Mets — for their logos, preside over front and end matter with an air of pinstripe refinement while allowing for the projectile antics of ovoid Mr. Met.

Marketing modern luxury, classic elegance, and Old World charm, eclectic polyglot variations of script typeface still flourish in Manhattan. Consider Saks Fifth Avenue, Century 21 department store, the Booth Theatre, Emilio's Ballato, P.J. Clarke's, John's Pizzeria, El Quijote, Citarella's, Murray's Sturgeon Shop, Junior's Cheese Cake — *New York* magazine itself.

Mathew Carter's 1972 rendition recalls a style of handwriting favored by the English writing master George Shelley. Due, if only in part, much to Shelly's successful promotion in England, his Round Hand had spread by mid-18th century throughout Europe and crossed the Atlantic to North America. There, finally, like one of every three from abroad and every other somewhere else in the United States, it arrived in New York.